Steck-Vaughn Company
   Executive Editor   Diane Sharpe
   Senior Editor   Martin S. Saiewitz
   Design Manager   Pamela Heaney
   Photo Editor   Margie Foster
   Electronic Cover Graphics Alan Klemp

Proof Positive/Farrowlyne Associates, Inc.
Program Editorial, Revision Development, Design, and Production

Consultant: E. Cameron Reeder, Information Specialist, Communications Division, Bureau of Tourism and Travel

Published by Raintree Steck-Vaughn Publishers, an imprint of Steck-Vaughn Company.

A Turner Educational Services, Inc. book. Based on the Portrait of America television series by R. E. (Ted) Turner.

Cover Photo: Cover photography of the State Capitol by © John Elk/Tony Stone Images.

Library of Congress Cataloging-in-Publication Data

Thompson, Kathleen.
   Alabama / Kathleen Thompson.
      p.   cm. — (Portrait of America)
   "Based on the Portrait of America television series"—T.p. verso.
   "A Turner book."
   Includes index.
   ISBN 0-8114-7321-X (library binding).—ISBN 0-8114-7426-7 (softcover)
   1. Alabama—Juvenile literature. [1. Alabama.] I. Title. II. Series:
Thompson, Kathleen. Portrait of America.
F326.3.T48 1996
976.1—dc20
                                95-25725
                                  CIP
                                  AC

Printed and Bound in the United States of America

   4 5 6 7 8 9 10 WZ 03 02 01 00

Acknowledgments
The publishers wish to thank the following for permission to reproduce photographs:
P. 7 © Jim Schwabel/Southern Stock; p. 8 © Dan Brothers/Alabama Bureau of Tourism & Travel; pp. 10, 11 North Wind Picture Archive; p. 12 Montgomery Area Chamber of Commerce, Convention & Visitors Division; p. 13 The Photographic Collections of the Birmingham Public Library; p. 14 (both) University of South Alabama Photographic Archives; p. 16 The Photographic Collections of the Birmingham Public Library; p. 17 (top) The Photographic Collections of the Birmingham Public Library, (bottom) AP/Wide World; p. 18 AP/Wide World; p. 19 Birmingham Convention & Visitors Bureau; pp. 20, 21 Library of Congress; p. 22 Tuskegee Institute; p. 23 (top) New Farm Photo, (bottom) Tuskegee University; p. 24 © Jim Schwabel/Southern Stock; p. 26 (top) NASA, (bottom) Alabama Bureau of Tourism & Travel; p. 27 (top) Auburn University, (bottom) NASA; p. 29 (top) Alabama State Parks, (bottom) Birmingham Convention & Visitors Bureau; p. 30 University of Alabama at Birmingham; pp. 31, 32 Alabama Bureau of Tourism & Travel; p. 34 (both) Russell Cave National Monument; p. 35 (top) Birmingham Convention & Visitors Bureau, (bottom) © Michael Reagan; p. 36 (top) Alabama Bureau of Tourism & Travel, (bottom) AP/Wide World; p. 37 (top) Alabama Bureau of Tourism & Travel, (bottom) U.S. Army Aviation Museum; p. 38 AP/Wide World; p. 39 Alabama Bureau of Tourism & Travel; p. 40 Courtesy Kathryn T. Windham; p. 41 (both) Courtesy Mrs. Rosa Miller Hobbs Joyce; p. 42 University of Alabama; p. 44 © Jeff Greenberg/Southern Stock; p. 46 One Mile Up; p. 47 (left) One Mile Up, (center) © Will & Deni McIntyre/Photo Researchers, (right) Alabama Bureau of Tourism & Travel.

STECK-VAUGHN

PORTRAIT OF AMERICA

Alabama

Kathleen Thompson

A Turner Book

RSVP

RAINTREE
STECK-VAUGHN
PUBLISHERS

The Steck-Vaughn Company

Austin, Texas

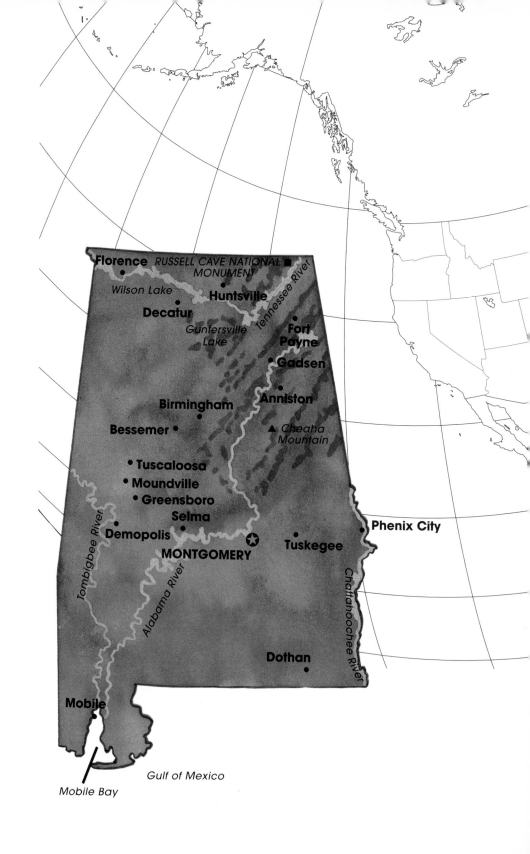

Alabama

Florence • RUSSELL CAVE NATIONAL ■
MONUMENT

Wilson Lake
Huntsville •

Decatur •

Guntersville
Lake

Tennessee River

Fort
Payne •

Gadsen •

Anniston •

Birmingham •

Bessemer •

▲ Cheaha
Mountain

• Tuscaloosa

• Moundville

• Greensboro

Selma •

Tombigbee River

Demopolis •

MONTGOMERY ★

Tuskegee •

Phenix City

Alabama River

Chattahoochee River

Dothan •

Mobile •

Gulf of Mexico

Mobile Bay

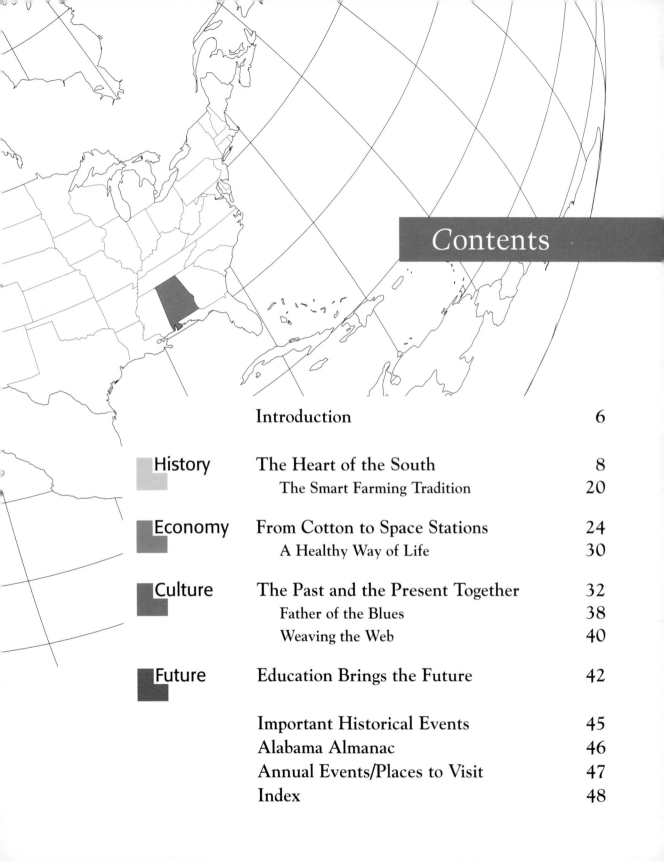

Contents

Introduction

Alabama's landscape varies from sandy shores along the Gulf of Mexico to swampland to black-clay farmlands. The state also has rolling hills, deep pine forests, and mineral-rich limestone valleys. Even though the shape of the land may change, wherever you go in Alabama, you'll find things growing. This lush, green land brings forth beautiful flowering trees and shrubs. Farmers raise cotton, corn, oats, wheat, and peanuts. Wild Spanish moss laces the trees in the swamplands. Orchids, goldenrod, and magnolias bloom in the forests and the fields. Natural wonders thrive in Alabama. It's a land of variety, vegetation, and vitality.

These fishing boats provide a colorful foreground to Dauphin Island, near the mouth of Mobile Bay.

Alabama

camellias, Heart of Dixie, farming

The Heart of the South

When Europeans arrived in the Alabama region, four groups of Native Americans had already been living there for hundreds of years: the Cherokee, the Chickasaw, the Choctaw, and the Creek. They built permanent log homes, and they grew corn, squash, beans, and tobacco. They hunted deer and other animals and fished in the area's rivers.

In 1540 the Spanish explorer Hernando de Soto led a force of more than five hundred into the Alabama region. They were traveling south looking for gold. De Soto fought with almost every Native American group along the way. In Alabama he and his troops battled Choctaw Chief Tuskalusa and his warriors at Mabila, north of today's Mobile. When the battle ended, several thousand Choctaw were dead. Almost twenty years later, Tristán de Luna and several hundred settlers arrived in the Mobile area. By 1561 they had abandoned their settlement.

Almost 140 years passed before Europeans returned to the Alabama region. But events outside

The Boll Weevil Monument in Enterprise honors the beetles that ate most of the South's cotton crop in 1915. The loss caused Alabama farmers to learn they could make more money raising other crops.

Spanish explorer Hernando de Soto explored present-day Alabama by following the river valleys south to what is now Mobile.

the region would affect it later. The English had settled into 13 colonies along the East Coast, and they also claimed all the land to the west of them. In 1682 French explorer René-Robert Cavelier, Sieur de La Salle, had completed his exploration of the Mississippi River and claimed the entire Mississippi River basin for France. He called the new land Louisiana after the French king Louis XIV. England immediately contested this claim.

To defend its rights to Louisiana, France built a chain of forts from Canada to the mouth of the Gulf of Mexico. In 1702 two French brothers, Pierre Le Moyne, Sieur d'Iberville, and Jean Baptist Le Moyne, Sieur d'Bienville, founded Fort Louis on the Mobile River in present-day Alabama. Fort Louis was an outpost for traders and a home for new settlers. It was the first permanent European town in the Alabama region. It was also the capital of Louisiana. In 1711 severe flooding almost destroyed the fort, so it was moved to a safer place closer to the mouth of the Alabama River. When the settlement at present-day New Orleans became the new capital of Louisiana in 1720, Fort Louis was renamed Fort Condé.

Years of skirmishes between the French and the British finally turned into a full-fledged war in 1754. It was called the French and Indian War because many Native American groups fought alongside the French against the British. Great Britain won the war and gained control of most of the land east of the Mississippi River. The British took over Fort Condé and renamed it Fort Charlotte.

Starting in 1764 Great Britain began taxing the people of the colonies to help pay the expenses of fighting the war. The colonists declared their independence from Great Britain in 1776, resulting in the Revolutionary War. In 1779 Spain became an ally of the colonists by joining in the war against Great Britain. Spain hoped that the British would lose the war, and Spain would gain more territory. In that year Bernardo de Gálvez captured Fort Charlotte and Mobile for Spain.

In 1783 the American colonies won their independence from Great Britain. Because Spain was an American ally, Spain received an area that included the port city of Mobile and some land north of there. In 1795 Americans negotiated with Spain and gained the region north of Mobile. In 1806 the Cherokee, the Chickasaw, and the Choctaw gave up large sections of their land through treaties with the United States government. American settlers started to move into the region.

In 1812 war broke out again between the United States and Great Britain. In an important battle in 1813, American forces seized Mobile from Spain. The United States now claimed all of Alabama. That same year a group of Native Americans called the Red Stick Creek attacked and killed several hundred settlers at Fort Mims. The Red Stick Creek had also attacked other Native American settlements. The next year troops led by General Andrew Jackson joined with the White Stick Creek, the Chickasaw, the Choctaw, and the Cherokee to defeat the Red Stick Creek at the

At the Battle of Horseshoe Bend, Andrew Jackson's army of two thousand defeated a force of eight hundred Creek. The peace terms awarded the United States 23 million acres of Creek land in present-day Alabama and Georgia.

Battle of Horseshoe Bend. In the end Jackson forced the Red Stick Creek and the groups that had fought beside him to give up most of their land to the Americans.

By 1817 Alabama had enough settlers to become a territory. Two years later Alabama became the twenty-second state. Many Alabama farmers had created plantations along a section of the state called the Black Belt, named for its rich, black-clay soil. Plantation owners used slaves to plant, care for, and harvest cotton, the major crop in Alabama and throughout the South.

Growing cotton was very profitable in Alabama. Farmers wanted more land to plant their crops, so they put greater and greater pressure on the government to move the remaining Native Americans off the land. President Andrew Jackson signed the Indian Removal Act of 1830. It stated that all Native Americans east of the Mississippi River should be "removed" to land in present-day Oklahoma. Federal troops came into Alabama to forcibly remove all Native American groups to the West. The route taken by the Cherokee became known as the "Trail of Tears"

Jefferson Davis and his family lived here, in the first "White House" of the Confederacy, located in Montgomery.

because so many Cherokee died from hunger, cold, and exhaustion.

A national debate over slavery was growing louder by the 1840s. There was no doubt about which side most Alabamians supported. In 1848 the Democratic state convention adopted the Alabama Platform, which said that the federal government had no right to bar slavery in any new territory. By 1860 slaves made up nearly half the population of Alabama.

Abraham Lincoln was elected President in 1860. In his campaign speeches, Lincoln had promised to keep slavery from expanding in the United States. Southerners believed that his election threatened their way of life. One by one, Southern states seceded, or withdrew, from the United States. In 1861 Alabama seceded and changed its name to the Republic of Alabama. The state then invited the other Southern states to a convention in Montgomery to form a new country, the Confederate States of America. The members drew up a constitution and declared Montgomery the capital. Later that year Virginia

In the background of this drawing sits the state house in Montgomery. After representatives had voted to form the Confederacy, they elected Jefferson Davis to be President and made Montgomery the capital.

top. Rear Admiral David Farragut led the Union Navy in the Battle of Mobile Bay. The force was led by two iron-clad ships that had gun turrets on their decks. The other ships in the fleet were wooden sailing ships.

above. Rear Admiral David Farragut was in such poor health at the time of the Battle of Mobile Bay that he tied himself to the rigging of his flagship in order to continue fighting.

seceded from the Union, and the capital was changed to Richmond, Virginia.

Alabama sent around 110,000 soldiers to fight in the Civil War. The most important battle in Alabama took place at the Confederate port of Mobile in 1864. The Union Navy was led by Rear Admiral David Farragut, a Southerner who chose to fight for the Union. Several captains were afraid to enter Mobile Bay because it was filled with floating mines, then called torpedoes. Admiral Farragut shouted, "Damn the torpedoes, full speed ahead!" The Union fleet moved in and won the battle.

The Confederates surrendered in 1865. The period after the Civil War was called Reconstruction. This was the process created by the federal government to readmit the former Confederate states into the Union. Among the government's goals during Reconstruction was to guarantee the rights of freed slaves. The government also attempted to help Southern states rebuild their economies. However, by 1873 Alabama was $32 million in debt.

Reconstruction did bring some needed reforms to Alabama. African Americans gained many rights, including the right to vote. Not all people supported those rights. Some who didn't joined organized groups such as the Ku Klux Klan. The Klan terrorized African Americans, burning down their homes and sometimes even killing them. In 1874 southern Democrats regained control of Alabama's government. They quickly passed a new constitution and a series of laws that took away almost all of the African Americans' newly won rights.

Reconstruction was a tense period for the South's economy, as well as for its people. Agriculture, especially cotton, was still important in Alabama. But after the war, there was no money to hire workers, so landowners designed a system called "sharecropping." Under this system plantations were divided into small farms, and sharecroppers rented the farms and grew crops. The owners sold the crops and paid a small percentage of the profit to the sharecroppers. Low earnings made it impossible for sharecroppers to move up to a better life.

In 1915 a plague of insects called boll weevils devastated the cotton fields of the Black Belt. When their farms failed, many African Americans left Alabama to find work in the North. They left in even greater numbers after the United States entered World War I in 1917. Northern cities needed laborers to work in factories building war materials. At the same time, Alabama farmers grew more food to feed the troops. Also, shipbuilding was established in Mobile.

Before the cotton harvest was mechanized, picking cotton was back-breaking work.

The 1930s was the era of the Great Depression in the United States. Banks and factories closed, and people lost their savings. In 1933 President Franklin D. Roosevelt created the New Deal, a series of agencies and projects designed to put people back to work. Alabama farmers received money and instruction in both soil conservation and new agricultural methods. The Tennessee Valley Authority was a New Deal project that oversaw the building of dams along the Tennessee River.

These dams, besides lowering the occurrence of flooding, produced inexpensive electricity for everyone in the region. By the end of the 1930s, Alabama had three TVA dams. The inexpensive power helped industries grow more quickly. These changes improved the standard of living in Alabama.

When the United States entered World War II in 1941, industries used the electricity provided by TVA projects to produce war materials. The Redstone Arsenal was constructed in Huntsville to design and develop rockets for the war. Once again the war effort created more jobs in Birmingham's steel mills and in Mobile's shipbuilding industry. Alabama farms produced food for troops overseas.

After World War II ended in 1945, most of the country experienced an economic boom. But life for African Americans changed very little. Alabama laws still prevented most African Americans from voting.

Segregation laws forced African Americans to use separate schools, restaurants, and even elevators.

In 1954 the United States Supreme Court stated that segregated schools were unconstitutional. Then, in 1955 Rosa Parks, an African American woman, was riding home from work on a Montgomery bus in the back section reserved for African Americans. All the seats in the front were filled, so a white man told her to stand so that he could sit down. She refused and was arrested. This incident led Dr. Martin Luther King, Jr., the minister of the Dexter Avenue Baptist Church, to organize a city-wide boycott against the Montgomery bus system. A year later the federal courts ordered the buses desegregated.

At the same time, Alabama had to face other racial problems, especially its segregated schools. In 1963 the federal courts ordered the state to allow five African American students to enroll in the University of Alabama. The governor, George Wallace, tried to stop the action. But President John Kennedy called out the National Guard, so Wallace backed down. The same thing happened when African American students tried to enter a Montgomery public high school. Events elsewhere in the state were

Many women in Alabama and across the country worked in factories during World War II, producing airplanes and other materials for the war effort.

Rosa Parks became nationally known when she refused to give up her seat on a bus to a white man.

not as peaceful, especially in Birmingham, where police sometimes resorted to violence to enforce Alabama's segregation laws.

Many African Americans in Alabama could not vote because of laws that discriminated against them. To protest this discrimination, in 1965 Dr. Martin Luther King, Jr., led 25,000 people in a five-day march from Selma to Montgomery, the state capital. That year Congress passed the Voting Rights Act, making it illegal to stop African Americans from registering and exercising their right to vote.

As many Alabamians moved from farms to the cities, there was an increase in the demand for government services, such as education. To pay for such services, the state increased taxes on cigarettes and alcohol in 1980. The economy got a boost in 1985 when the Tennessee-Tombigbee Waterway, a 234-mile canal, connected two of the state's main river systems.

Dr. Martin Luther King, Jr., (left) was awarded the Nobel Peace Prize in 1964 for his civil rights efforts.

This Birmingham museum exhibit honors Dr. Martin Luther King, Jr., who used nonviolent methods to promote civil rights for African Americans.

This made it easier to move products to the port in Mobile.

As industries grew and the population increased during the 1980s and early 1990s, Alabamians began working on ways to make energy less expensive. The price of oil and gas rose, so Alabama worked to develop its coal deposits more fully. In 1991 the first-ever compressed-air electrical energy plant in the United States opened in Alabama. The plant generated energy that was 25 percent less expensive and 67 percent cleaner than standard power plants.

Alabamians have set their feet on the path of advancement. The state has created special offices and organizations to attract new businesses and raise the income of its people. More jobs and a higher quality of life is Alabama's goal as it prepares for the challenges of the twenty-first century.

The Smart Farming Tradition

Before the Civil War, it was illegal to teach any slave how to read and write. This became a serious problem for many African Americans after the war because they didn't have the education necessary to succeed in a free society. In 1875 Alabama adopted a new constitution that allowed African Americans to be educated as long as schools were segregated. One of the schools that provided advanced education for African Americans was Tuskegee Normal and Industrial Institute, which opened in 1881. Tuskegee Institute, as it is usually called, was set up to provide elementary and secondary education to its students.

The first leader of Tuskegee Institute was Booker T. Washington. Washington was born a slave, and he knew how hard the lives of former slaves could be. When he was nine years old, he had to go to work in the coal mines and salt furnaces in West Virginia. Later, he worked his way through college by attending classes during the day and working as a janitor at night. When Washington finished college, he became a teacher.

In 1881 Washington began to run the institute. At first the school was more a wish than a reality—it began in an abandoned church. But Washington believed in his project, and he set up specific goals. He felt it was essential that African Americans gain the practical vocational skills that they needed in order to prosper in their work. So Tuskegee Institute began training people in trades such as carpentry, mechanics, and farming. The school also trained teachers. More and more buildings were built, and Washington searched for the best teachers he could find.

Booker T. Washington (front, center) was the head of Tuskegee Institute for 33 years, until his death in 1915.

At that time, more Americans worked on farms than anywhere else. Researchers at Tuskegee Institute concentrated on ways to increase the amount of money farmers could earn from their farms. So in 1896 Washington hired George Washington Carver, one of the greatest scientists of the time, to be the head of the agriculture department at Tuskegee Institute. Carver had also been born a slave, and he too had known hard times. He had worked his way through school and specialized in agricultural research. Carver was the perfect choice for Washington's growing institute.

Carver turned his attention to important agricultural issues such as soil conservation. At that time farmers in Alabama grew only cotton, a plant that took many nutrients from the soil. Carver knew that if people continued to grow nothing but cotton, the soil would become worn out. It wouldn't grow any crops at all. Plus, a farmer who depended on only one crop could lose everything if it was attacked by insects or disease. In one season a farmer could be ruined completely.

Carver conducted research on crops that farmers could grow instead of cotton. He was especially interested in sweet potatoes, soybeans, and peanuts. Like cotton these plants used nutrients, but they also returned nutrients to the soil. And they were very useful. Over the years Carver found more than three hundred ways to use the peanut plant! It could be used to make coffee, flour, ink, dyes, and substitutes for cheese and milk. Carver

George Washington Carver taught classes as well as did research at Tuskegee Institute.

also found more than one hundred uses for sweet potatoes. Tuskegee Institute became famous because of the work that Carver did.

Today, this school is known as Tuskegee University, and it is no longer segregated. But Tuskegee continues to be concerned with the problems faced by today's farmers. For example, it has become harder for small farms to compete with large farms, even with crops such as peanuts and soybeans. So at Tuskegee, researchers like Dr. Booker T. Whatley and others have followed the tradition of Washington and Carver—they are working to solve current farming problems.

Whatley proposed that small farmers should specialize by growing crops such as grapes or blueberries. Large farmers aren't interested in these crops because the plants require too much individual care. Grape growers must prune each vine individually to get a good crop. Then, when the grapes are ripe, the clusters must be picked by hand. Large farmers prefer to rely on machines, such as threshers that harvest wheat, rather than picking crops by hand.

Lately researchers at Tuskegee have looked into ways in which plants can be grown in outer space. These harvests would provide healthy diets for people working and living in a space station.

Tuskegee has broadened its mission from its early years when it was looking for a replacement crop for cotton. Its commitment to agriculture has continued, however. With farm-land currently diminishing, the ability to grow crops in many kinds of climates may become even more important in the future. Tuskegee researchers have kept in mind that fresh food is the key to health—whether it is in outer space or right here on Earth.

Dr. Booker T. Whatley poses with the statue called "Lifting the Veil of Ignorance" at Tuskegee University. The statue honors Booker T. Washington.

Tuskegee Institute became Tuskegee University in 1985. It offers bachelor's and master's degrees as well as a doctoral degree in veterinary medicine.

From Cotton to Space Stations

Beginning about 1792 Alabama grew cotton and almost no other crop. In 1910 the cotton crop—and the economy—was devastated by an insect called the boll weevil. This insect invaded Alabama's cotton fields, destroying farm after farm. By 1915 almost 90 percent of the crop was lost.

Alabama farmers had no choice but to grow other crops. They raised corn, soybeans, peanuts, and wheat. They also raised poultry and livestock. By growing a number of different crops, Alabama farmers hoped to prevent experiencing anything like the boll weevil crisis again.

Today, Alabama has a diversified economy. That means the economy relies on many industries. Service industries make up almost two thirds of Alabama's economy. The largest groups of service industries are retail trade and wholesale trade. Retail trade means selling items to an individual buyer. Wholesale trade is selling products to a business, usually in large quantities. Especially important to Alabama's economy are

Alabama is still considered part of America's cotton belt, but the state's largest crop is soybeans. More farmland is planted with soybeans than with cotton.

A space shuttle engine is tested at Redstone Arsenal in Huntsville.

wholesale businesses that trade in groceries, machinery, and mineral products. That's because Alabama also produces these kinds of products.

Government services make up 15 percent of the economy. This category includes anyone who works for the city, county, state, or federal governments. The military is especially important to the state's economy. Alabama is the home of major military bases for all of the armed forces.

The Redstone Arsenal became the home of the Marshall Space Flight Center in 1960. The center is a part of the National Aeronautics and Space Administration (NASA). Its scientists developed the *Saturn* V rocket, which would go to the moon a few years later. Alabama has continued to be a center for space projects, from the Lunar Roving Vehicle and the Hubble Space Telescope to the orbiting space station.

Community, social, and personal services are also part of the service economy. These include operations such as hospitals, counseling services, and law offices. Finance, insurance, and real estate are also important categories of the service industry. So are transportation, communications, and utilities, which include trucking, railroads, oil and natural gas pipelines, and shipping.

Mobile has the tenth largest port in the country. About two hundred shipping companies have

The Blessing of the Shrimp Fleet is an annual event at Bayou La Batre.

their headquarters in Mobile. The port provides shipping to and from every major port in the world. Mobile imports, or receives, agricultural products, such as tropical fruit, from other countries. Alabama also imports raw materials needed for its factories, including bauxite, rubber, and iron ore. Products exported, or shipped to other countries, from the port at Mobile include coal, chemicals, iron and steel products, agricultural products, and many high-tech products. More than eighty thousand people in Alabama have jobs that depend on the shipping industry.

above. These men are working at one of Alabama's catfish farms.

below. NASA launched the space shuttle *Discovery* in 1990. The Marshall Space Flight Center in Huntsville developed the propulsion system used in all of the space shuttles.

Alabama turned to manufacturing earlier than many states in the South. Even before the Civil War, Alabama mined iron ore and turned it into products such as railroad tracks. In 1880 the first blast furnace opened in Birmingham and began producing steel. By the 1890s iron and steel manufacturing was the leading industry in the state.

Today, manufacturing accounts for about 22 percent of Alabama's economy, but iron and steel play minor roles. Instead paper products—pulp and paper, cardboard, paper bags, and paper tissue—are the leading products of the state's manufacturing economy. Alabama also produces chemicals and textiles. Most manufacturing takes place in northern Alabama.

The military's needs—especially in the area of space research—also have contributed to Alabama's

economy. Since World War II, high-tech manufacturing industries—businesses that develop computers, robots, and lasers—have settled in Alabama. High-tech jobs help the economy because they pay well and require people with special skills.

High-tech industries also provide instruments and machines that medical researchers and doctors use. Medical research is very important in Alabama—especially genetic research and the development of new ways to diagnose and treat illnesses.

Mining makes up two percent of Alabama's economy. There are oil and natural gas reserves in the state, but coal is becoming more important. Coal is a less expensive source of energy than oil and other petroleum products. Limestone, bauxite, and marble are other mining products.

Farming isn't as important in Alabama as it used to be. Agriculture accounts for about two percent of Alabama's economy. Most of the farms are in central and southern Alabama. Today, cotton accounts for only two percent of the farm output. The major agricultural products are livestock, corn, peanuts, pecans, and soybeans. Poultry is by far the largest livestock income producer. Chickens amount to about 40% of all farm products sold in Alabama.

Alabama's beautiful and varied landscape and its Gulf of Mexico coast provide the state with another important source of income—tourism. People come to explore the southern reaches of the Appalachian Mountains and to swim and fish in Alabama's lakes and rivers. Visitors also enjoy touring the many

De Soto Falls is located near Fort Payne. Natural features such as this attract a large number of tourists to Alabama each year.

restored plantations in the southeastern section of the state.

Alabama draws visitors to two particular sports, golf and automobile racing. Two major automobile races, the Winston 500 and the DieHard 500, take place in Talladega. The International Motorsports Hall of Fame is also located there. Alabama's dedication to golf may be even greater than to racing, however. Alabama has developed the Robert Trent Jones Golf Trail, a string of golf courses from the northern to the southern regions of the state. The trail draws golfers from all over the world because of the variety of the courses. The courses range from hilly in the north to flat in the south. In addition to the golf trail, there are about one hundred courses in various Alabama communities.

Alabama has changed a great deal since the days when its economy relied solely on cotton. At that time plantation owners were the only people who had any wealth. Today, through a diversified economy, Alabama has increased the prosperity of all of its people.

Birmingham is one of Alabama's industrial centers.

A Healthy Way of Life

Technology is extremely important in medicine today. Not so long ago, doctors and medical assistants had only the X-ray machine to help them see hidden, solid body structures like bones. Now health care workers also use CAT scans and MRIs to reveal soft-tissue structures such as the brain and the heart. High-tech microscopes use lasers and other techniques to reveal extremely small structures—sometimes single atoms! Who knows what secret medical research will uncover next?

No one knows the answer to that question, but the latest inventions are in the planning stages in Alabama. The number of high-tech medical facilities in the state is growing rapidly. Many of Alabama's medical facilities are in Birmingham. The Southern Research Institute (SRI) is a leader in the research on cancer and AIDS. It also studies the effects of air pollution. There are only six other institutes in the country that can match the scope of research that is conducted at SRI. The medical center complex at the University of Alabama at Birmingham (UAB) is one of the top medical centers in the United States. UAB is a research and treatment center for cancer, arthritis, infectious diseases, and vision disorders. It also has one of the top dental schools in the nation. Besides UAB there are 23 other hospitals or medical centers in the city. They specialize in areas such as pregnancy, heart problems, and emergency services.

Medical researchers such as Dr. Charles Bugg hope to find cures for today's incurable diseases.

Twelve thousand Alabamians work at the Medical Center at the University of Alabama at Birmingham. The Medical Center is Birmingham's biggest employer.

Dr. Charles E. Bugg is a member of the medical treatment and research community in Birmingham. He is the former director of the Center for Macromolecular Crystallography at UAB. Now Dr. Bugg and several other scientists have formed their own research company, BioCryst Pharmaceuticals Inc., which develops disease-fighting drugs.

Employing X rays and advanced computers, Dr. Bugg and the medical researchers at BioCryst use what they know about protein molecules to design medicines that will attack specific diseases. In fact the research team can create medicines that are designed for a specific person!

Medical centers and research companies like Dr. Bugg's are important to Alabama's economic health. In 1994 almost forty thousand people in Birmingham worked in hospitals or for other companies involved in medical research. By working to find cures for diseases such as cancer and AIDS, the Birmingham medical establishment is bringing about another kind of well-ness—good economic health. That's one kind of health care we all need.

The Past and the Present Together

Stories, songs, folk dances, and fairs are all part of a place's culture, or way of life. Culture also includes the fine arts—symphonies, paintings, sculpture, literature, classical dance, and museums. Culture includes history and the way it affects people's lives. Culture in all of these forms can be found in Alabama.

Large cities, such as Birmingham and Montgomery, are centers for the fine arts in Alabama. Every spring Birmingham holds the Festival of the Arts, one of the oldest continuous festivals in the United States. It is considered among the ten best arts festivals in the country. Montgomery's Alabama Shakespeare Festival attracts 250,000 visitors every year. These theatrical productions have received national and international praise. The Mobile Museum of Art has almost five thousand works of art. Throughout the state there are smaller groups that strongly support the arts.

Alabama's history is a rich one. It begins with the people who lived in the region thousands of years ago. Near Bridgeport is Russell Cave, a national monument

Stately Kendall Manor in Eufaula is typical of the many restored historic homes that showcase Alabama's past.

that contains artifacts of Native American life dating back more than eight thousand years. Another people, the Mound Builders, are commemorated at Moundville Archaeological Park. It includes twenty flat-topped mounds, many artifacts, and a rebuilt village. There are other Native American sites all around the state, such as Historic Blakeley Park near Mobile, which includes a number of mounds. Historic Blakeley Park also includes an early French and Appalachee Native American settlement from the early 1700s.

Alabama's parks, museums, and festivals all recognize the influence of the early days. At one time or another, Spain, France, and Great Britain all claimed the region as their own, so each country left evidence of their presence. Fort Condé, the first fort on Mobile Bay, is one example. Guides at Fort Condé dress as French soldiers and lead visitors through the building that has housed French, Spanish, British, and American troops over the centuries. On display are reproductions of cannons and other materials left by each group.

Plantation life is also remembered in Alabama. Most of Alabama's great plantations were burned down during the Civil War, but those that remained have been restored. The Buena Vista Mansion in Prattville is one of those places. When a building is restored, people try to repair, paint, and furnish it so that it looks the same as when it was first built. In the Buena Vista Mansion, that meant preserving a remarkable 24-foot-high circular staircase. It reaches from the first floor to a banquet room on the third floor. Outside, the gardens are filled with the same types of flowers that bloomed there before the Civil War. Some of the restorations, such as Magnolia Grove in Greensboro, also include smaller buildings on the grounds.

Alabama's culture was profoundly shaped by the Civil War. In cities such as Selma, Florence, and Montgomery, there are museums and monuments to Civil War battles. The most famous battle took place on Mobile Bay where two forts, Fort Gaines and Fort Morgan, defended the outlet into the Gulf of Mexico. Every year Alabamians reenact this battle at Fort Morgan, which was the southernmost Confederate fort. Other reenactments take place in other parts of the state.

Sloss Furnaces National Historic Landmark is a monument to Birmingham's industrial history. These furnaces produced pig iron for almost ninety years.

Many mansions built before the Civil War tell us about the grand lifestyle that cotton and slavery brought plantation owners.

The technique of basket weaving and other handicrafts in Alabama has been handed down over many generations.

Harper Lee's book *To Kill a Mockingbird* was the basis of a celebrated movie made in 1962.

Alabama's writers draw on the past, too. Harper Lee is an Alabama writer who wrote about the problems that arose from segregation and slavery in her novel *To Kill a Mockingbird*. This book told about the troubles between the races in a small Alabama town. The novel was awarded the Pulitzer Prize for Literature in 1961. This was the first time a Pulitzer was won by a writer from Alabama.

Alabama was the setting for the civil rights movement of the 1950s and 1960s. The Civil Rights Memorial in Montgomery is a constant reminder of the struggle by African Americans and other Americans to enforce the constitutionally guaranteed right of equality. The memorial was designed by Maya Lin, who also designed the Vietnam Memorial in Washington, D.C. The Civil Rights District in Birmingham includes the 16th Street Baptist Church, where a 1963 bombing caused the deaths of four African American girls attending Sunday school. Similar monuments to the civil rights movement are found throughout the state.

Alabama's culture isn't limited to its past, however. It also includes areas of special interests, such as flying and space travel. Wilbur and Orville Wright started their first flying school in Montgomery, Alabama. Today, at that very spot, people can visit the Monument to Powered Flight at Maxwell Air Force Base. Near Huntsville the United States Space and

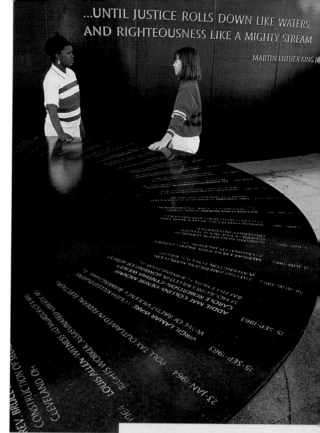

...UNTIL JUSTICE ROLLS DOWN LIKE WATERS AND RIGHTEOUSNESS LIKE A MIGHTY STREAM

MARTIN LUTHER KING Jr.

Rocket Center features exhibits that include the Saturn rockets as well as a lunar lander. There are more than sixty hands-on exhibits at the center, so people can experience the sights, sounds, and gravity forces of a real space flight!

Culture also comes from people's everyday lives—and that includes music. The "father of the blues," W. C. Handy, was born in Florence, in the northwest corner of Alabama. Today, Handy's home is a museum where people can see his handwritten compositions, his piano, and other memorabilia. Country and western music has deep roots in Alabama, too. It is the home of musicians, such as Hank Williams, Tammy Wynette, and the band Alabama. The state celebrates its musical heritage at the Alabama Music Hall of Fame in Tuscumbia and in annual festivals.

Culture acts as an identity for a group of people. What serves as culture is not selected by the people, but rather comes about through their actions. The pride Alabamians have in their past, their appreciation for the present, and their hope for the future make up a unique identity— one that bears the stamp of Alabama.

above. Maya Lin designed the Civil Rights Memorial in Montgomery as a tribute to the forty Americans who died during the civil rights movement from 1954 to 1968.

below. The United States Army Aviation Museum at Fort Rucker displays one of the largest helicopter collections in the world.

Father of the Blues

When William Christopher Handy was a little boy, he sometimes sat beside the Tennessee River outside his hometown, Florence. There he would listen to African American laborers singing as they worked. Their music was unusually expressive, combining feelings of sadness and joy. This kind of music left a lasting impression on Handy. He eventually adapted these sounds and melodies to create a form of music known simply as "the blues."

When he was 15 years old, W. C. Handy bought a trumpetlike instrument called a cornet and taught himself to play it. After graduating from high school, he left home hoping he could make his way in the world by playing music. He found the going was rough. For many years Handy traveled through towns such as St. Louis, Chicago, and Memphis, playing his cornet anywhere people were willing to pay him. Sometimes he played with other musicians at clubs or on street corners. Other times he played alone for the money people might toss to him. He often had no place to sleep. One night in St. Louis, Handy rested on a cobblestone walkway near the Mississippi River. He heard a lonesome

W. C. Handy is shown here at the age of 76 in his music publishing office. Although he lost his eyesight twenty years before his death, Handy continued to make frequent appearances at concerts and benefits.

Visitors to the W. C. Handy Home and Museum can view Handy's trumpet, piano, and handwritten musical scores.

voice from somewhere in the dark say, "I hate to see that evenin' sun go down." The suffering behind the other man's words was not unknown to Handy himself.

In 1911 W. C. Handy successfully combined the folk tunes he learned as a child with the orchestral band music he played to earn his living. His first popular success was a campaign song he wrote for a Memphis politician named Crump. The song was so well liked that he rewrote the words, made a few minor changes, and called it "Memphis Blues." Three years later he wrote his greatest work, "St. Louis Blues." The opening lines of the song begin with the words he had heard at the river that night in St. Louis.

W. C. Handy wrote many classic blues tunes, including "Yellow Dog Blues," "Beale Street Blues," and "Joe Turner Blues." In 1918 he started his own music publishing firm called Handy Brothers Music Company.

Handy lost his eyesight when he was 57 years old. Even though he was blind, he published and produced music until his death in 1958. W. C. Handy's legacy includes more than 150 songs. The rich, emotional music he created has endured throughout the years, establishing him in history as the "Father of the Blues."

Weaving the Web

Kathryn Windham grew up in the Alabama storytelling tradition. Storytelling is an art. A good storyteller knows how to look at everyday people and really see them, really appreciate them, and really understand them. Storytellers catch the little examples of behavior that tell so much about a person. For instance Windham remembered a pair of sisters who were just a little odd. Just one example tells us a great deal about these two women. "I think about the Fallon sisters and how they talked to each other out loud during church. They were elderly women and deaf and did not realize how loud they were talking. They'd say, 'How much longer's he going to preach, sister? It's time we went home.'"

Storytellers are like historians or photographers. They record what happened and to whom it happened so that the rest of us can learn about the past. Rosa Miller Joyce learned her stories from her grandmother. Grandmother Hobbs, who lived to be 96 years old, had lived through the Civil War. Joyce remembers one

Storyteller Kathryn Tucker Windham learned her art from her father, who was, she said, "the finest storyteller I ever heard."

remarkable story told by her grandmother.

Grandmother Hobbs was a young woman when the Union soldiers marched through Alabama. As they came they burned crops in the fields and looted homes, often burning them down. The soldiers targeted wealthy Southerners especially, and the Hobbs family was wealthy. Since the men were all off at war, there was only Grandmother Hobbs to protect the house. She knew she couldn't stop the soldiers, but she thought maybe she could outsmart them.

So Grandmother Hobbs put the family silver in jewelry bags and

This photo shows the home Grandmother Hobbs protected during the Civil War.

hung the bags on hooks within the walls. Then she gathered the family jewelry and sewed the pieces into special pockets in her petticoat. However, she knew that the soldiers would wonder where the jewelry was. So she filled the safe with cheap costume jewelry and then waited for the soldiers to come. When they did, she let them in.

Joyce remembers well what her grandmother said she did then. "She went over to that iron safe . . . wearing that quilted petticoat that contained

Grandmother Hobbs used a petticoat full of pockets to fool Union soldiers.

the really valuable pieces and worked the combination on the safe. I can still hear her voice as she told us about this. She passed the trays of these pieces around to the soldiers who were there, reaching out, and said, 'Take one! Take one! Give it to your sweetheart. Tell her you stole it in Dixie!'

"And I don't know why her sarcasm didn't let them in on her secret, but they thought she'd been generous with them. And as a result of what they considered her generosity, a guard was posted on this house. And it was not burned."

Today, Grandmother Hobbs's house still stands in Selma. Her granddaughter has kept it in much the same condition as when her grandmother was a girl. The house and the stories are part of what makes Alabama what it is today.

41

Education Brings the Future

As Alabamians move into the future, they face great challenges. Although Birmingham and Montgomery are thriving cities with new, high-tech industries and strong economies, there is still much poverty in the state. Breaking down that poverty will require a great deal of emphasis on education. In fact education is what is needed most for Alabama's future.

Today, Alabama has gained a reputation for encouraging high-tech industries and space research. Alabama industries manufacture instruments such as lasers and computer hardware and software. It will take high-tech skills to continue developing projects like these. The needed skills will only come from advanced education.

Alabama has a strong farming tradition. To continue that tradition, farmers must earn enough from their products. The best chance of that happening is through agricultural research. Higher education institutions, such as Tuskegee University, provide the environment for such research.

Alabama's 15 state-funded, four-year colleges have made a significant improvement on the quality of education in the state in recent years.

Preserving its rich natural environment is another challenge facing the state. The main economic reason for preserving the environment is tourism, which contributes a large percentage of Alabama's income. Also, Alabama's swampy wildlife reserves and national forests are treasures that Alabamians don't want to lose. Once again research and a thorough understanding of natural systems are needed to stem the further loss of natural areas.

Alabamians have a goal for the future. That goal starts with a step toward improved education.

This sunset over Mobile Bay brings the promise of fair weather and hope for a better tomorrow.

Important Historical Events

1000 Native Americans build mounds in western Alabama.

1200 Choctaw, Chickasaw, Cherokee, and Creek begin farming in Alabama.

1519 Alonso Álvarez de Piñeda sails into Mobile Bay. He is the first European to visit what is now Alabama.

1540 Hernando de Soto leads an expedition into present-day Alabama and battles the Choctaw.

1702 Pierre Le Moyne, Sieur d'Iberville, and Jean Baptist Le Moyne, Sieur d'Bienville, found Fort Louis.

1711 Flooding forces the relocation of Fort Louis to the present site of Mobile.

1720 Fort Louis is renamed Fort Condé.

1763 The French give up their claim to Alabama. The British take control of Fort Condé.

1780 Spain captures Mobile from Great Britain in the Revolutionary War.

1795 The Americans renegotiate the Treaty of San Lorenzo and gain much of what will be northern Alabama.

1813 The Americans seize Mobile Bay from the Spanish.

1814 General Andrew Jackson defeats the Red Stick Creek. The Creek cede their land to the United States.

1817 Alabama becomes a federal territory.

1819 Alabama becomes the 22nd state.

1861 Alabama secedes from the Union. Montgomery becomes the first capital of the Confederacy.

1864 Union and Confederate ships fight the Battle of Mobile Bay.

1865 Union cavalry invades Alabama. Robert E. Lee's army surrenders.

1868 Alabama is readmitted into the Union.

1881 Tuskegee Institute is founded.

1901 Alabama adopts its present constitution.

1929 Alabama is hit by serious flooding.

1933 The Tennessee Valley Authority is established to control flooding and bring jobs to the region.

1941 Redstone Arsenal is built in Huntsville.

1955 Rosa Parks is arrested when she refuses to give up her seat on a bus to a white man. Dr. Martin Luther King, Jr., leads a boycott against the Montgomery bus system.

1963 George Wallace becomes governor. In June and September, President John F. Kennedy sends the National Guard to enforce school integration.

1965 Dr. Martin Luther King, Jr., leads a march from Selma to Montgomery to advocate voting rights for African Americans. Congress passes the Voting Rights Act.

1982 George Wallace is elected for a record-setting fourth term as governor.

1985 The Tennessee-Tombigbee Waterway, a 234-mile canal, is opened, connecting two of the state's main river systems.

1993 The Alabama legislature declares the state's school-funding formulas unconstitutional, stating that they deny students in poor communities an opportunity to receive a solid education.

The state flag shows a red cross on a white background. The cross suggests the symbol of the Confederacy.

Alabama Almanac

Nickname. The Heart of Dixie

Capital. Montgomery

State Bird. Yellowhammer

State Flower. Camellia

State Tree. Southern pine

State Motto. *Audemus jura nostra defendere* (We dare defend our rights)

State Song. "Alabama"

State Abbreviations. Ala. (traditional); AL (postal)

Statehood. December 14, 1819, the 22nd state

Government. Congress: U.S. senators, 2; U.S. representatives, 7. State Legislature: senators, 35; representatives, 105. Counties: 67

Area. 51,718 sq mi (133,950 sq km), 29th in size among the states

Greatest Distances. north/south, 329 mi (530 km); east/west, 210 mi (338 km). Coastline: 53 mi (85 km)

Elevation. Highest: Cheaha Mountain, 2,407 ft (734 m). Lowest: sea level, along the Gulf of Mexico

Population. 1990 Census: 4,062,608 (4% increase over 1980), 22nd among the states. Density: 79 persons per sq mi (30 persons per sq km). Distribution: 62% urban, 38% rural. 1980 Census: 3,890,061

Economy. *Agriculture:* chicken, beef cattle, soybeans, peanuts, greenhouse and nursery products. *Fishing:* shrimp, oysters. *Manufacturing:* paper products, chemicals, primary metals, food products, clothing. *Mining:* coal, natural gas, petroleum, crushed stone, limestone

State Seal

State Flower: Camellia

State Bird: Yellowhammer

Annual Events

★ Mardi Gras celebration in Mobile (February/March)

★ Floral Trail/Dogwood and Azalea Festival in Auburn/Opelika (April)

★ Alabama June Jam in Fort Payne (June)

★ World Championship Domino Tournament in Andalusia (July)

★ Cherokee Pow-Wow and Green Corn Festival in Gadsden (August)

★ Pioneer Peanut Festival at Landmark Park in Dothan (October)

★ Riverfront Market/Tale-Tellin' Festival in Selma (October)

★ Blue-Gray Football Game in Montgomery (December)

Places to Visit

★ Birmingham Civil Rights Monument in Birmingham

★ First White House of the Confederacy in Montgomery

★ Fort Gaines Historical Site, on Dauphin Island

★ George Washington Carver Museum, at Tuskegee University

★ Ivy Green (Helen Keller's birthplace) in Tuscumbia

★ Moundville Archaeological Park

★ Russell Cave National Monument, near Bridgeport

★ U.S. Space and Rocket Center in Huntsville

Index